15 Ways to Nourish Your Faith

Susan Shannon Davies

Paulist Press
New York/Mahwah, New Jersey

Acknowledgments
Unless otherwise indicated, Scripture quotations used here are from the *New American Bible*, Copyright 1986, 1970, The Confraternity of Christian Doctrine, Inc. All rights reserved. Lyrics from "The News" are used with permission of the songwriter, Mary Hartman.

Cover/book design and interior illustrations by Nicholas T. Markell.

Library of Congress Cataloging-in-Publication Data

Davies, Susan Shannon, 1962–
    15 ways to nourish your faith / by Susan Shannon Davies.
        p.   cm.— (IlluminationBooks)
    Includes bibliographical references and index.
    ISBN 0-8091-3790-9 (alk. paper)
    1. Spiritual life—Catholic Church. I. Title. II. Series.
BX2350.2.D37   1998
248.4'82—dc21   98–14609
                                                              CIP

Published by Paulist Press
997 Macarthur Boulevard
Mahwah, New Jersey 07430

Printed and bound in the
United States of America

Contents

IlluminationBooks

A Foreword

W hen this series was launched in 1994, I wrote that Illumination-Books were conceived to "bring to light wonderful ideas, helpful information, and sound spirituality in concise, illustrative, readable, and eminently practical works on topics of current concern."

In keeping with this premise, among the first books were offerings by well-known authors Joyce Rupp *(Little Pieces of Light...Darkness and Personal Growth)* and Basil Pennington *(Lessons from the Monastery That Touch Your Life)*. In addition, there were titles by up-and-coming authors and experts in the fields of spirituality and psychology. These books covered a wide array of topics: joy, controlling stress and anxiety, personal growth, discernment, caring for others, the mystery of the Trinity, celebrating the woman you are, and facing your own desert experiences.

The continued goal of the series is to provide great ideas, helpful steps, and needed inspiration in small volumes. Each of the books offers a new opportunity for the reader to explore possibilities and embrace practicalities that can be employed in everyday life. Thus, among the new and noteworthy themes for readers to discover are these: how to be more receptive to the love in our lives, simple ways to structure a personal day of recollection, a creative approach to enjoy reading sacred scriptures, and spiritual and psychological methods of facing discouragement.

Like the IlluminationBooks before them, forthcoming volumes are meant to be a source of support—without requiring an inordinate amount of time or prior preparation. To this end, each small work stands on its own. The hope is that the information provided not only will be nourishing in itself but also will encourage further exploration in the area.

When we view the world through spiritual eyes, we appreciate that sound knowledge is really useful only when it can set the stage for *metanoia,* the conversion of our hearts. Each of the IlluminationBooks is designed to contribute in some small but significant way to this process. So, it is with a sense of hope and warm wishes that I offer this particular title and the rest of the series to you.

–Robert J. Wicks
General Editor, IlluminationBooks

Introduction

Y ou and I can choose to be holy. Not in a pious, holier-than-thou attitude, but in a deep, daily faith attitude. One that says, "I believe in and love Jesus, and therefore I am going to start acting like it in every detail of my life." Believe it or not, God has his hand in everything we do, and we can learn to discern his direction. That's what this book is all about–cultivating spiritual practices that help us listen to God.

No one else can do this for us. We walk hand in hand with the Lord. Others can support us, but the relationship is between each one of us and God. Nourishing our own spiritual growth requires a conscious decision. It is a daily act of will.

Do not store up for yourselves treasures on earth, where moth and decay destroys, and thieves break in and steal. But store up treasures in heaven, where neither moth nor decay destroy, nor thieves break in and steal. For where your treasure is, there also will your heart be (Mt 6:19–21). Every detail of our lives should be focused on God.

Because Jesus Christ calls us each to a unique path, no one spiritual practice will suit everyone all the time. Be open to change. This book will introduce you to some spiritual practices. Use them if and when they become important on your own journey. God loves to surprise us, so we need to be spiritually flexible.

We must know that our path will be different from anyone else's path. Each person draws close to the heart of God through entirely individual circumstances. The design of our spiritual walk is ultimately unique to our life in God. *As one face differs from another, so does one human heart from another (Prv 27:19).*

Keep in mind that all spiritual practices are meant to be a means to an end, not an end in themselves. Don't focus exclusively on any one way to pray. Any spiritual practice will be useless if it is not leading us to a deeper relationship with Jesus. We may find, for example, that meditation or journaling work well for certain periods in our spiritual journey and not in others. As long as we are keeping our heart focused on the love of Jesus, he can lead us to the practices that he knows will help us.

Then we can stand back and let the Author of Life

work. If we invite Jesus to change our hearts, he will. It won't happen because we are doing XYZ spiritual practice three times a week. The transformation will happen because God truly loves us and desires full union with us.

Union with God is the goal. Nothing else in life will ever completely satisfy. *So faith, hope, love remain, these three; but the greatest of these is love (1 Cor 13:13).*

For reflection

· If you were 80 years old, looking ahead to heaven and back on your earthly life, what would you wish you had done more of or less of?

· How would you finish this phrase? I want a deeper relationship with Jesus, but I...

· Reflect on and write down the story of your own spiritual history.

one
two
three

Chapter One

Daily Prayer

P*ray without ceasing.*
 –1 Thessalonians 5:17

The *Catechism of the Catholic Church* reminds us that "we cannot 'pray at all times' if we do not pray at specific times, consciously willing it."[1] In our busy lives, taking time for prayer is not always easy. *Train yourself for devotion, for while physical training is of limited value, devotion is valuable in every respect, since it holds a promise of life both for the present and for the future* (1 Tm 4:7–8).

Daily prayer nourishes us just as our daily meals feed us and keep us healthy. Mahatma Gandhi spoke profoundly about prayer: "Prayer is the key of the morning, and the bolt of the evening." Jesus cannot teach us to love him (and therefore pray unceasingly) unless we form the habit of praying regularly. Some form of daily prayer is the key to all other fruitful spiritual practice. It's like saying to God, "I am committed to you, no matter what my day or my life brings."

Jesus is our best role model in daily prayer. He prayed in ecstasy during the Transfiguration. He prayed in agony in the Garden. And he prayed at every time in between. The "every time in between" is when we also will do most of our praying.

Some people make a sincere effort to pray (turn attention toward Jesus) especially when doing mundane tasks like cleaning the toilet or vacuuming the floor. Many people pray at stoplights or in grocery checkout lines. Ordinary daily events can trigger moments of prayer in our lives.

To make room for prayer, reduce or eliminate TV time. Or try getting up twenty minutes earlier to be with the Lord before the day begins. *Fill us at daybreak with your kindness–that we may shout for joy and gladness all our days* (Ps 90:14). Many people motivate and remind themselves of their commitment to prayer by setting up a prayer corner somewhere in their home. They put their Bible, prayer books, some religious art, a crucifix, or a candle in the place where they pray. This helps set the tone for prayer.

Prayer does not have to be just petitions. Prayer can include times of praise and thanksgiving, liturgy, Scripture reading, silence, rosaries, vocal prayer, journaling, meditation, contemplation, adoration of the Blessed Sacrament, spiritual music, and other practices that turn our attention toward Jesus.

Just repeating the name of Jesus has a tremendous power to transform our own attitudes and outward situations. Frank Laubach spent his life trying to call Jesus to mind every second of every day. He reflected that in the beginning it was strenuous to do this, but soon everything else in his life became easier![2]

Listening to God means fostering a daily discipline of silence. God doesn't call most of us with a lightning bolt like he did St. Paul. And our modern lives are literally bombarded with noise from lawn mowers, television, radio, cars, appliances, and telephones. We can close the door on that noise at least once a day.

It is important to remember that the devil is never happy with our daily prayer efforts. "Prayer is a battle against ourselves and the wiles of the tempter who does all he can to turn us away from prayer, away from union with God."[3] In *The Screwtape Letters*, C. S. Lewis provides insight into the subtle ways the devil attempts to disrupt our walk with God. The whole book is a series of letters from a senior devil (Screwtape) to a junior devil (Wormwood) who has been "assigned" to a man who is teetering in his commitment to God. In one of the letters, Screwtape advises Wormwood to divert the man with mundane things like his hungry stomach when he starts pondering spiritual matters too deeply. Ordinary earthly things can divert us from prayer and listening for God.

The daily commitment to prayer, the habit of just doing it, is the beauty of this spiritual practice. Perseverance—even when emotions don't feed us, even when we don't see the benefits, even when we are tempted to spend the time doing other things—will lay the foundation for a nourishing, fruitful journey.

It is often at the times when we seem to be moving in slow motion or standing still spiritually that God does his most efficient work in our souls. And remember that God does the work in us—we simply provide the fertile soil by structuring our lives toward openness to him.

Jesus can nourish each one of us through regular daily prayer. "To pray unceasingly is to sense that our thirst for God is as great as God's thirst for us."[4] *Have no anxiety at all, but in everything, by prayer and petition, with thanksgiving, make your requests known to God. Then the peace of God that surpasses all understanding will guard your hearts and minds in Christ Jesus* (Phil 4:6-7).

For reflection

• What do you have to give up in order to make room for prayer?

• Do you fear closeness with God? What are those fears? How might the devil be using those fears to keep you from a deeper prayer life?

• Read the Gospels and reflect on a verse in which Jesus is praying.

Chapter Two
Eucharist

I am the living bread that came down from heaven; whoever eats this bread will live forever; and the bread that I will give is my flesh for the life of the world.

–John 6:51

In the Catholic tradition, Holy Communion is at the center of faith. It is the spiritual food, literally the body and blood of Jesus, that feeds and nourishes us. It is the sign of the covenant God has made with his people. *The cup of blessing that we bless, is it not a participation in the blood of Christ? The bread that we break, is it not a participation in the body of Christ? Because the loaf of bread is one, we, though many, are one body, for we all partake of the one loaf (1 Cor 10:16–17).*

Jesus is truly present in the bread and wine. Priests have reflected that if we honestly believed that, then we would be flocking to daily and Sunday mass in droves. We would make time in our busy lives to receive our Lord in his body, blood, soul, and divinity.

People have shared that being away from weekly Eucharist is like being spiritually malnourished. Prayer becomes more difficult when we aren't being fed by the body of Christ. Nothing but union with Jesus will satisfy us. We have a God-shaped space in our hearts that cannot be filled by anything else. We find nourishment for our souls when we return to the eucharistic table.

When we spend time with people who are holy, something of their presence rubs off on us. We take something of the atmosphere around them with us. It's the same with Jesus. When we spend time in adoration of the Blessed Sacrament or at mass, we absorb Jesus. We learn to know him just by being with him. Many people say that adoration makes a big difference in their spiritual lives. A weekly adoration hour is one of the few times during the week when we can sit in silence and be fully conscious of Jesus' presence.

Just as we need the body and blood of Jesus, so too we need the communal aspect of liturgy. When Jesus began his ministry, he immediately formed a community. He did not walk his road on this earth alone, and neither should we. Coming together once a week (or more) with a community is necessary for support. *Where two or three are gathered together in my name, there am I in the midst of them* (Mt 18:20). It nourishes our faith to have regular contact with other Christians.

Ideally, our eucharistic liturgy should be a common prayer—a celebration and overflow of our own personal walk with the Lord. "By its very nature the liturgy is meant to be a coming together to express and deepen faith so that the sending forth at the end of the liturgy can be for the building up of the Church and living lives of Gospel witness in the world."[5] Community worship and Eucharist are meant to be embedded in our daily lives, an integral part of our spiritual journeys.

"In a very real sense we, who receive the Bread of Life, become the Bread of Life for others."[6]

For reflection

• What is the most important result of Eucharist in your own life?

• Read 1322–1405 in the *Catechism of the Catholic Church*.

• Look up and reflect on one of the eucharistic passages (Mt 26:28; Lk 24:35; Jn 6:35; Jn 6:47–57; 1 Cor 11:23–29).

Chapter Three

Scripture Study

*I*n the beginning was the Word,/and the Word was with God,/and the Word was God.

–John 1:1

The Word of God is the anchor of the spiritual life. A beautiful, mysterious thing happens when we read the Bible daily. *I will place my law within them, and write it upon their hearts* (Jer 31:33). The powerful words become etched in our deepest being. Without even trying, we begin to make decisions through the invisible filter of Scripture.

Reading the Bible regularly has the power to nourish us beyond our wildest dreams. In his book *Healing*

Through the Mass, Robert DeGrandis describes how Scripture changed a prison inmate's life. This man was up for parole after many years in prison. He was not a Christian, but he decided that he might have a better chance at parole if he could show that he was making an attempt to change his life. So he picked up a Bible and read it cover to cover—many times. Slowly, almost against his will, he found himself changing. His whole attitude about his life changed. By the time the parole hearing came around, he really had become a Christian.[7]

This man wasn't even looking for God. How much more can the Word of God nourish us when we are looking for spiritual food! *Indeed, the word of God is living and effective, sharper than any two-edged sword, penetrating even between soul and spirit, joints and marrow, and able to discern reflections and thoughts of the heart* (Heb 4:12).

Attending daily mass or doing the daily readings is a great way to let God feed us. Many people memorize short Bible selections daily or weekly. Being able to recall the Word of God helps us to know the mind of God. Kimberly Hahn, in her book *Rome Sweet Home*, reminds us that God can give us sweet consolation in times of distress by bringing to our minds particular passages of Scripture. But he can't do that if we haven't taken the time to memorize it in the first place.[8]

Families can search the Scripture for verses to memorize. They can write them on little cards, read them at breakfast, and try to recall them throughout the day. Then at dinner, the verse can become part of the prayer before meals. *One does not live by bread alone, but by every word that comes forth from the mouth of God* (Mt 4:4).

Formal Bible study can also deepen our faith. Not only does this broaden our knowledge of the historical context and theological implications, but small group sharing can deepen our own awareness of the way God moves in our lives and in the lives of others.

Perhaps the most intense, personal way to read the Bible is called *lectio divina* (holy reading) or reading with the heart. We don't read this way to get information. Instead, we read so that God's Word can touch and change us. When we are touched by a word, a phrase, or a whole passage, we stop and dwell on it.

God's Word is spiritual food for us. Just like with a nice meal, we let our reading be leisurely. Then we can enjoy the taste and sound of the words. We can read some parts out loud or reread sections several times. God has special messages for us through *lectio divina.* We can think of them as vitamin tablets formulated perfectly for our spiritual nutritional needs.

For example, we might read Matthew 14, where Jesus has just finished feeding the five thousand. After dismissing the people and his disciples, *he went up on the mountain to pray.* We might reflect that we too need time to go to the mountain to pray in order to sort out the voices we hear every day. Hearing the voice of God above our own voice, the voices of well-meaning family and friends, and the voices of the world is a difficult thing. Even Jesus needed quiet time to discern his Father's voice.

...the rain and snow come down from heaven,/ and do not return there until they have watered the earth,/making it bring forth and sprout,/giving seed to the sower and bread to the eater,/so shall my word be that goes out from my mouth;/it shall not return to me empty,/but it shall accomplish that for which I purpose, and succeed in the thing for which I sent it (NRSV, Is 55:10–11). God's Word has a definite purpose and tremendous power.

For reflection

- Take one of the parables in the Gospels and read it with your heart. What is Jesus teaching you from your reading?
- When you hear or read a scripture verse that has meaning, do you reflect on it or write it down or share it with a friend?
- What are some biblical principles that you try to live by?

four

five

six

Chapter Four

Reconciliation

W*e implore you on behalf of Christ, be reconciled to God.*
—2 Corinthians 5:20

Regular reviews of our thoughts and conduct are important if we are seeking the kingdom of God. Sin is sometimes so ingrained in daily life that we don't recognize it until we begin a consistent, honest evaluation process.

God can bring to our awareness little habits (and big ones) that erect a wall between us and his grace. If we simply ask, the Holy Spirit will begin to move in our hearts to show us what we need to work on. *Good and upright is the LORD;/ thus he shows sinners the way./He guides the humble to justice,/*

he teaches the humble his way./All the paths of the LORD are kindness and constancy/toward those who keep his covenant and his decrees (Ps 25:8–10).

Human nature is basically self-centered and childish. We want what makes us feel good, what feeds our ego. This is the struggle in walking with God. Even Jesus wrestled with this human condition in the Garden. *Father, if you are willing, take this cup away from me; still, not my will but yours be done* (Lk 22:42). Submitting our will and selfishness to the Father is the only remedy for this dilemma.

The sacrament of Reconciliation provides a wonderful vehicle for facilitating this process. "Indeed the sacrament of Reconciliation with God brings about a true 'spiritual resurrection,' restoration of the dignity and blessings of the life of the children of God, of which the most precious is friendship with God."[9] Maybe if we were really using the sacrament the way it could be used, our society wouldn't need so much psychotherapy!

Dennis and Matthew Linn, in their book *Healing of Memories,* reflect that "confession offers everyone power to love and grow. Confession is like nourishing food or medical care...often used to sustain and speed up the healing process."[10] They don't recommend that the sacrament be just a laundry listing of offenses, but more a vehicle for Christ to enter and heal those hurts and emotional "garbage" that cause us to sin.

Inner healing is based on the idea that sin springs out of our emotional woundedness. If we can allow Jesus to heal the hurts, then we can reduce or eliminate our dependence on sin as a coping strategy. Sometimes we can't even remember the wounds that can happen at any stage of our lives.

For example, if a mother secretly didn't want to be pregnant, that could cause deep emotional pain in the developing baby, and that wound might predispose the child to sinful behaviors like rage or unhealthy expectations of others. Through inner healing and reconciliation Jesus can enter and heal that wound of being unwanted. Nothing else on this earth can erase that kind of trauma.

With that idea, the Linns recommend three steps in preparation for a healing confession. First, we thank God for healing and progress made since our last confession. Second, we discern and confess what Christ wants healed. Concentrating on just one troublesome area of our life will help us be specific. And third, we surrender painful memories to Christ for healing. With any sin, there will be multiple times when each root memory caused pain or trouble. We then allow those thoughts and memories to surface and surrender them to Christ's healing love.

In addition to the sacrament, we can do a daily examination of conscience. Our loving Father, in his wisdom, will show us, a little at a time, the areas that need refining and purging. This process may be painful, but it may be the only way to make room in our souls for the divine love that God so desperately wants to share with us. Forgiveness of both ourselves and others can help clear the channels that connect us to God's grace. *Therefore, since we are surrounded by so great a cloud of witnesses, let us rid ourselves of every burden and sin that clings to us and persevere in running the race that lies before us while keeping our eyes fixed on Jesus, the leader and perfecter of faith* (Heb 12:1–2).

Try praying Psalm 139 with a sincere heart. Allow the presence of God to settle deep within your soul: *Probe me, O God, and know my heart;/try me,/and know my thoughts;/See if my way is crooked,/and lead me in the way of old* (Ps 139:23–24).

For reflection

• Pray Psalm 139 before your next examination of conscience.

• What little habit of yours might be getting in the way of a relationship with Jesus?

• Define humility. Notice what the Bible teaches about it (Sir 3:17–28; Eph 4:2; Col 3:12; 1 Pet 5:5–7).

Chapter Five

Entertainment

W hatever is true, whatever is honorable, whatever is just, whatever is pure, whatever is lovely, whatever is gracious, if there is any excellence and if there is anything worthy of praise, think about these things.

–Philippians 4:8

There is one overriding rule for turning our spiritual and physical eyes toward God: how we choose to spend our time will dictate how deeply we can journey inward. If we spend four hours every day watching sitcoms on television, we limit God in our lives. Books, music, television, and movies provide subtle, yet powerful stimuli toward or away from God.

Does our reading material provide real spiritual food for our journey? Are romance novels our life's passion? Or blood-and-guts drama? There are so many books in libraries and bookstores—fiction and nonfiction—that will draw us closer to God. Religious bookstores and sections of bookstore chains are replete with inspirational, spiritual, prayerful reading material. Quality spiritual reading material nourishes us as individuals and as a community.

St. Teresa of Avila hungered after deep spiritual books, and they can feed our spirits as well. Lives of the saints also provide nourishment for the mind and spirit.

...[S]ing psalms and hymns and spiritual songs among yourselves, singing and making melody to the Lord in your hearts... (NRSV, Eph 5:19). We can also choose our music based on whether it will draw us closer to the Lord. Classical and inspirational music can do this. So can Christian radio and music. Today's Christian music is upbeat and inspirational. Having the car radio tuned in regularly to a Christian station keeps us focused on God's Word and on fellowship with the Lord.

If what we choose to spend our energy on is critical to advancing in the spiritual life, we need to avoid music that contains subtle negative messages. Christian, inspirational, and classical music is appropriate and appealing for young and old. Whole families can enjoy the benefits of listening to Christian music.

Consider limiting or eliminating television viewing. Americans waste so many hours each week watching television. If you want to reduce your television time, try this exercise. Make a list of what you regularly watch. Cut it in half. Then choose only those programs that will help you move closer to all that is good. Chances are, if you are honest in your evaluation of each program, you won't be left with a long list.

Think how much time that will free up for spiritual or family goals. Limiting the family's viewing to wholesome, family-oriented programs that uplift and entertain is a big part of making room for God in our lives. Excessive television viewing doesn't leave time for spiritual reading, meaningful conversation with family members, hobbies that might draw us closer to Jesus, setting an example of a healthy daily routine for our children, or quiet time to just "be." Too much time is dictated by what shows are on. We can't go to bed at 9:23 if we are tired, because we get locked into a show that doesn't end until 10:00.

We can think of limiting television like limiting junk food. If we are striving to include mostly nutritious foods in our diet, there won't be much room for junk food. When we replace television with more spiritually nourishing activities like daily prayer or spiritual reading, we will notice a great improvement in our satisfaction with life and with our relationships.

Even entertainment that seems neutral can draw us away from the love of God. If something isn't drawing us closer to the Lord, then it must be pulling us away. We need to structure our lives to be filled with positive, lifegiving experiences. *Do not conform yourself to this age but be transformed by the renewal of your mind, that you may discern what is the will of God, what is good and pleasing and perfect* (Rom 12:2).

For reflection

• What are some influences in your life right now that don't draw you closer to God?

• What are the influences that do draw you closer to God?

• Jesus didn't speak specifically about television in the Bible, but there are some biblical principles found there (examples: humility, honesty, unselfishness, generosity). Analyze a couple of television shows with your family to discover what biblical principles they espouse.

Chapter Six

Journaling

*T*here are also many other things that Jesus did, but if these were to be described individually, I do not think the whole world would contain the books that would be written.

—John 21:25

A friend wrote a song called "The News" that puts all the books of the Bible to music. It's a great help in memorizing the order. The song includes these words:

The last verse of the book of John,
it says I could write on and on,

but I doubt if there'd be enough room in the world to hold
the whole of the holy word. You and me,
we got to tell the story,
the Bible left untold,
our lives got to be the pages the whole world could not hold.[11]

It's a powerful image: that our lives are truly a part of the story of God. It didn't end when sacred scripture writers stopped their writing. Jesus continues to work in the world today and in our lives. Just as the Bible reviews the lives of the Jews, of Christ, and of the early Christians, we can review our individual spiritual progress with a journal. Prayer happens while we are writing of spiritual things. This record can truly help to steer our spiritual journey.

A journal can be a record of dreams, meditations, prayer requests, thoughts, Bible verses, inspirational quotes, struggles, and any other life experiences. We can structure entries as letters to Jesus.

We don't need to worry about grammar, spelling, or sentence structure. A journal is not subject to an English teacher's scrutiny. We write from the heart and allow our deepest thoughts expression. It's not of great concern if anger, disappointment, or hurt find their way into our writing. Seeing negative emotions in print can be a catalyst for Jesus' healing.

There are no hard-and-fast rules about how often to write in a journal. Some people write once a day, once a week, or even once a month. Others like to write only as

the Spirit moves them or the need arises. At first, to culti-
vate the habit, we may need to schedule a time to write
once a day or once a week. Making it a part of daily prayer
time might help.

A spiral notebook will work, as will a blank book
specifically designed for journaling. The date should pre-
cede each entry. Keeping the journal next to the bed is
handy for recording dreams (see chapter 10). Remind family members that even though a journal may be accessible,
they need to respect each other's privacy.

A periodic rereading will refresh our memories of
spiritual lessons. Something written three months or ten
years previously may help confirm God's leading in our
current situation. It may make us laugh or cry. It may give
us goosebumps as we begin to see connections that would
be invisible in any other format. It will reassure us of the
definite movement of God in our lives— even though on
any given day, we may not *feel* God's presence.

Morton Kelsey calls a journal a sacrament of the
inner life, a symbol of the religious quest. In his words:
"My journal has kept me honest, given me companionship
and allowed me to listen to the deepest levels of myself,
allowed me to vent my deepest anger, and brought me into
creative, saving relationship with the heart of reality,
whom I have found to be a Divine Lover, Love Divine, all
loves excelling."[12]

*Keep my commands and live,/my teaching as the
apple of your eye;/Bind them on your fingers,/write them on the
tablet of your heart* (Prv 7:2–3).

For reflection

    • If you haven't done so yet, write your own faith history as if you were writing it to a future or present grandchild.

    • How are your friendships with other people aided by writing letters?

    • Keep a journal for a month or two and then evaluate its impact.

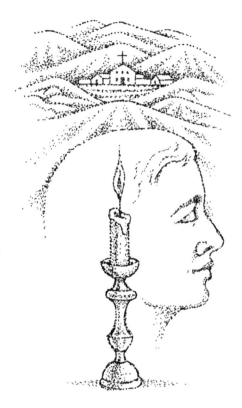

seven
eight
nine

Chapter Seven

Retreats

I *n those days he departed to the moun-*
tain to pray, and he spent the night in
prayer to God.

–Luke 6:12

Jesus found nourishment for his spirit in time
spent away from the daily pressures of his ministry. In a
world of media bombardment and financial pressures,
silence is a precious commodity. But it is one of incredible
value if we can foster it not only in short daily prayer but
also in regular retreat time away.

There are several types of retreats to consider:
group/thematic, directed, silent, self-guided, and Ignatian
30-day. Periodic long retreats are helpful because it takes

two to three days to unwind from the daily routine and stress. We can go to a retreat house, a monastery that provides retreat facilities, a friend's cabin in the mountains; or we can even stay home (provided no one else is there).

With some types of retreats, we just need to show up. With others, especially a self-guided retreat, we may need to gather some material, books, or special prayers in preparation. With any type of retreat, we can prepare ourselves in advance. Prayer that we will be open to the grace of God while on retreat makes a good preparation. We can also reflect on our reasons for going on retreat, trying to keep expectations at bay. Fasting beforehand for a short period can help us turn our hearts toward God.

The busier we are, the more apt we are to need a retreat. It's one of those apparent paradoxes of the spiritual world. The more time we are spending with God, listening to God, the more efficient we will be in our daily tasks.

A listening heart must be a joy to the Lord. He longs to fill our deepest being with his love, but we must make room and listen. Retreats are an excellent way to relax, unwind, and clear away room for God. We can think of them as a spiritual gift we give ourselves.

In his book *The Recollected Heart*, Philip Zaleski describes it like this: "Retreat...is a richly textured affair, harboring something of exploration, something of escape, and something of life-and-death struggle."[13] "During retreat, we stitch together, with the needle of silence and the thread of stillness, our scattered sense of self and our fragmentary experience of God."[14]

We may be fearful of time alone with God. When

we recognize this fear, we can be assured that progress is being made in our spiritual awareness. It is indeed a *fearful thing to fall into the hands of the living God* (Heb 10:31). This fear, acknowledged, is a stepping stone toward a fuller surrender to love.

Surrender requires losing ourselves, relinquishing our entire being, in order that God may have his way with us. And that can be scary. Releasing our will to the will of God is painstaking and hard work. It requires God's help. Annual or biannual retreats are an excellent way to come face to face with God—to let his will take deeper root in our hearts. Only then can we really become the people God intended us to be.

Retreats can help us find the spirit of retreat right in our daily lives. If union with God is the goal, then ultimately every moment can be like a retreat. We may never reach that state of perfection here on earth, but it's worth reflecting on and reaching for.

In the following Old Testament story, God is speaking to Elijah:

> Then the LORD said, "Go outside and stand on the mountain before the LORD; the LORD will be passing by." A strong and heavy wind was rending the mountains and crushing rocks before the LORD–but the LORD was not in the wind. After the wind there was an earthquake–but the LORD was not in the earthquake. After the earthquake there was fire–but the LORD was not in the fire. After the fire there was a tiny whispering sound *(1 Kgs 19:11–12).*

And the Lord was in the whisper. Our experience of God will likely be the same.

For reflection

- Reflect on any previous retreat experience you have had.
- Does time away with God appeal to you or scare you (or both)? Why?
- What type of retreat might suit you best right now?

Chapter Eight

Meditation

A nd Mary kept all these things, reflecting on them in her heart.

—*Luke 2:19*

Meditation is good for the body and for the soul. The health benefits are well documented. But when we add a spiritual dimension, we give God the opportunity to show us his truths. "Meditation is above all a quest.... Meditation engages thought, imagination, emotion, and desire."[15] God has given us the ability to pray with our imaginations.

In Christian meditation, the goal is unity with the living God. We need to select reading material and spiritual direction based on that principle. Morton Kelsey's book *The Other Side of Silence: A Guide to Christian Meditation* provides sound, biblical Christian guidelines on meditation. He suggests several aids to settling into the silence of meditation: use of a journal, controlled breathing, a small group of like-minded people or a prayer partner, a spiritual director, dreams, meditative reading, the Jesus prayer, and the use of images.[16] "Silence can open a door on a new dimension of reality. It is like finding a trap door or a secret passage, giving a way out of our usual, ego-dominated existence."[17]

For many of us, the idea of exercising our imaginations may be foreign. We may have a vague memory of using it when we were young, but we may have been told by parents or teachers that "daydreaming" would not be tolerated. But it's just this childlike freedom that meditation relies on. As adults, we can learn to recapture the atmosphere of imagination.

Any activity like painting, storytelling, dance, or imaginative writing can be the jumping off point for using our imaginations in prayer. Each person will find meditation and its fruit in a unique way. Once we find a couple of ways that provide a conducive atmosphere, we can relax and listen to the messages that come to us from our psyche and from God. Perseverance and practice are vital to success.

Simple meditations can be done by getting into a comfortable position in a place without distractions. We can imagine ourselves in a meadow or a chapel, or we can visualize ourselves in the presence of Jesus. A Bible passage can provide the scene for meditation. We can imagine ourselves as one of the characters or simply as an onlooker.

Recording or sharing with another person what happens, especially in our first attempts, may make it seem more real.

It's easy to worry that the images and results are something we just made up with our minds, and sometimes that may be the case. But with practice we will begin to experience things that don't come from our minds. For instance, in one person's early attempts at mediation, she imagined herself standing next to a beautiful creek with Jesus standing beside her. For a time, nothing happened. But then Jesus turned to her and held out his hand. In it was a seed, and she understood that he wanted to plant it with her next to the creek. When it was over, she marveled at how the meditation really had come to life, because she would never have been able to imagine Jesus with a seed to plant. Morton Kelsey reflects that "images are more like living beings with a life and purpose of their own."[18]

Personal encounters like these provide us with a deep awareness that Jesus is intimately interested in every detail of our lives and is quite willing to be present to us in our imaginations. Not only do we feel refreshed by times of meditation, but we also take valuable spiritual insights with us as well. A journal can be a valuable tool in recording these insights.

Meditation should not be undertaken lightly. It's not for everyone. A strong daily prayer foundation, a spiritual director, a circle of spiritual friends, and a stable daily routine will help us discern if it is for us. The spiritual world, like the physical world, is full of both darkness and light. However, God is in our imaginations. He can teach us about his love and care through meditative prayer.

Teach me, O LORD, your way/that I may walk in your truth;/direct my heart that it may fear your name (Ps 86:11).

For reflection

• What comes to your mind when you think about meditation?

• Have you read any secular books on meditation? What do you remember from them?

• Take a familiar scripture story and read it slowly. Sit in a quiet room and visualize yourself as one of the characters. Close your eyes and let the story unfold.

Chapter Nine

Contemplation

*R*ather, I have stilled my soul,/hushed it like a weaned child./Like a weaned child on its mother's lap,/so is my soul within me.

—Psalm 131:2

Contemplation is a simple gaze of faith. God wants to mold each one of us into the person we really are. And while God can use any life experience to do that, contemplation must be one of his favorite ways. Gazing on the Lord in utter silence requires some effort, but it is there that he can truly speak to our deepest souls.

We don't look for any spiritual or emotional experience during contemplation. We simply learn to rest in

God. The benefits of this form of prayer come in the rest of our lives. After beginning to practice contemplation, we may notice an improvement in our relationships with family members or coworkers.

As human beings, one of the best gifts anyone can give us is the gift of time and friendship. Our friendships need time, common experience, and love to grow and flourish. Even more is this true of our relationship with God. Desiring God, desiring the depths of his love is the proper motivation for contemplation.

The *Catechism* has this advice: "One does not undertake contemplative prayer only when one has the time: one makes time for the LORD, with the firm determination not to give up, no matter what trials and dryness one may encounter."[19] This is even more true in contemplation than in meditation. At least in meditation, we engage our imagination to aid our prayer. In contemplation, we seek to rest in God without visualization or images. We can't turn off our minds, but we can foster disinterest in the busyness of our thoughts. When they pull us away from contemplation, we simply let the thoughts go and return to God without fanfare.

M. Basil Pennington, O.C.S.O., and others actively promote a vehicle for contemplation called centering prayer.[20] Simply sit in a comfortable chair, relax, and enter the silence of the heart. In centering prayer, we choose a prayer word—something simple, like *Jesus*. Any short word will work. Whenever our thoughts intrude on the silence, we gently repeat our prayer word. Our minds will continue to work, but we don't become emotionally involved in any of our thoughts.

We can think of the arena of spiritual practices as being like a large pond that contains both large and small fish. At feeding time the smaller fish jump excitedly for the food. In contrast, the larger fish sit contentedly on the bottom, knowing they can get food whenever they need it. Contemplation is like being one of those large fish—content to sit quietly even while the activity of our thoughts continues all around us.

Two, twenty-minute centering prayer sessions are generally recommended per day. However, less time is better than no time. One person stuck to the twenty-minute routine for a time after first learning centering prayer. But then it became a chore, so she looked for another way. Now she centers for a few minutes every day or so, sometimes several times a day, and that works for her. As with any spiritual practice, we have to find our own best routine.

We don't look for any experience or gift from God during these times. Just being present to him is the idea. We let him have our full attention, just as we do with our closest friend. Jesus wants to be that close and that present to us. But like with our friends, we need to make time to be with him.

If you can, stop reading right now and have a centering prayer session.

To complement this type of prayer, Father Pennington recommends at least ten minutes a day of *lectio divina* or holy reading of Scripture. The Gospels especially can feed our souls and nourish our prayer time (see chapter 3).

It is rather reassuring that except for making the commitment to practice contemplation, we can't ensure its success by the force of our own will. God must do the work in our souls. Only God knows what needs to be done, so we can absolve ourselves from any responsibility to make anything happen.

The silence of contemplation is quite counter to human nature. Thomas Merton's advice is to "be still and let God work in you."[21] That goes contrary to our culture, which rewards activity and visible progress, and we are probably so used to noise and distraction that settling into that silence may be difficult at first. Yet eventually it can be a release, a blessed release from so much busyness and movement. Rest in it. Savor it. Come away from contemplation refreshed.

Setting aside a room in a quiet house with a comfortable chair for the practice of contemplation can be helpful. A candle, an open Bible, or another image may help to set the mood and the atmosphere of prayer.

We can also practice *noisy* contemplation in stolen moments in the middle of a hectic day. Acknowledging the silence of God or the presence of God or the greatness of God (with our prayer word) recommits us to him. Then we continue on with our day.

How lovely is your dwelling place,/O LORD of hosts!/ My soul yearns and pines/for the courts of the LORD (Ps 84:2–3).

For reflection

    • What images come to mind when you think about silence?

    • How could centering prayer benefit your prayer life?

    • Centering prayer can be done in a group too. You can teach it to a few friends or to a Bible study group.

ten

eleven

twelve

Chapter Ten
Dreams

Y*our sons and your daughters shall prophesy,/your young men shall see visions,/your old men shall dream* dreams.

–Acts 2:17

The Old and New Testaments are full of stories of God's providing direction and messages to people through their dreams. In many cultures and many historical times, holy people have respected and used their dreams as communications from the living God. They can be a rich source of inspiration and revelation.

In several of their books, Morton Kelsey and John Sanford discuss and promote a Christian approach to using dreams for spiritual enrichment. Dreams are another way of listening to the spirit world. In our dreams, we are not limited to the material world. Some say that our dreams can give us a glimpse of the freedom we will have upon reaching heaven.

We will not have visions from God every night. But when we are open to listening and respecting the power of dreams, we will begin to learn a great deal about ourselves. And those lessons can be applied to our spiritual walk with Jesus.

John Sanford pictures it like this: "Human development is like a tree that must be rooted in the earth in order to grow. The problem of our time is that we are like uprooted trees. Our roots no longer extend down into the inner depths to nourish us, so our growth cannot reach upward into the realm of the spirit. Our task [is to] see how dreams are like roots that reach far down into the nourishing depths of the earth of our souls, and help energy flow upward so our growth and development are possible."[22]

We have to train ourselves to remember and write down our dreams. A journal is a perfect place to keep this ongoing record of the deepest recesses of our being. A cassette tape player left next to the bed can also work.

Be consistent. Record everything, even if it seems insignificant (those things are often the most significant). Just the act of recording and paying attention to our dreams will increase our recall and our ability to interpret our dreams. If we structure our lives so we aren't so stressed and busy, then we can relax and listen to those messages from God and our deepest selves that come in dreams.

After recording your dreams, think about them and share them with a friend or relative who won't belittle or interpret them. Talking about them can often spark further recall and insights that weren't previously apparent. Think about the basic idea of the dream and about each individual element or symbol. What do they mean to you personally?

The only person who can know if a dream interpretation is right is the dreamer. It will just feel right. Sometimes no interpretation presents itself, and then we may just have to wait. Many dreams have meaning only after some time has passed.

We can pray with or about our dreams as well. Pray for an open heart and a listening spirit. Symbols and situations from dreams can become the basis for meditations. For instance, any dream that ends prematurely because of fear is a perfect candidate for a meditation prayer. We can visualize the beginning of the dream and then imagine Jesus standing right beside us. As the dream unfolds, the meditation will likely take on a life of its own and provide rich insight into some aspect of our spiritual walk with Jesus.

Not all dreams are glorious visions of God, but most contain some valuable wisdom and markers about where we are in our spiritual lives. Each one of us has this wonderful resource within us. With a little practice and an open heart, we can use our dreams to provide knowledge and inspiration that we cannot get in any other way.

John Sanford postulates that our subconscious has a picture of the person God created, the person that we will be when we finally meet our Creator, and that our dreams give us glimpses of that picture and also show us how we can become more like that person.

I will remember you upon my couch,/and through the night-watches I will meditate on you:/That you are my help,/and in the shadow of your wings I shout for joy (Ps 63:7–8).

For reflection

• Can you remember a dream that had a special impact on you? What made it special?

• When reading Scripture, note how many times God speaks in dreams and visions in both the Old and New Testaments.

• Tonight as you are going to sleep, ask God to help you remember any important dreams in the morning. When you wake up, write the dream(s) down.

Chapter Eleven
Spiritual Companions

*T*herefore, encourage one another and
build one another up, as indeed you
do.

−1 Thessalonians 5:11

In a world caught up in technology, money, and
status, it is easy to lose sight of what it means to be a Christian family. People need to talk with one another about
spiritual matters. We need to share our faith journey with
other Christians.

There are three parts to a healthy spirituality. One
is personal daily prayer, another is community worship,
and the last is small group prayer. Coming together weekly
or monthly helps us stay focused on Jesus Christ. These

groups might be in the form of scripture study, prayer groups, faith communities, or small circles of close friends.

St. John of the Cross says this about spiritual friendships. If they are truly from God, as your friendship deepens and grows, so will your love for the Lord. If they are not from God, they will draw us away from the source of life.[23] "Spiritual friendship is not an end in itself; it leads to growth in intimacy with others and God."[24] This gives us a simple formula for evaluating our friendships with individuals and groups.

Frequent the company of the elders;/whoever is wise, stay close to him (Sir 6:34). At some points during our spiritual journey, we may also find ourselves wishing for a spiritual director or spiritual companion—someone who has some experience in the inner way who can help guide us. This person can help us keep our feet on the path that leads to unity with God.

"The Holy Spirit gives to certain of the faithful the gifts of wisdom, faith and discernment for the sake of this common good which is prayer *(spiritual direction)*."[25] Realizing that traditional spiritual direction may not be as easy to find nowadays or that it may not even be the right model for some people, Father Thomas Legere proposes that we broaden our definition of spiritual direction. He suggests these images: companion, soul friend, guide, midwife (his favorite), spiritual friend, prophet, physician of the soul, leader of a mountain-climbing expedition, spiritual counselor, and lightning rod.[26]

As a community of churches, we would do well to help our members link up with someone else who can serve in one or more of these functions. Maybe we need to also provide formal training for those called to be spiritual companions. *We must consider how to rouse one another to love and good works. We should not stay away from our assembly, as is the custom of some, but encourage one another, and this all the more as you see the day drawing near* (Heb 10:24–25).

Each one of us would do well to keep our eyes focused on the LORD, so that if he needs to use us to be a short- or long-term spiritual companion or friend to someone else, we will not lead the person astray. *Admonish the idle, cheer the fainthearted, support the weak, be patient with all... always seek what is good for each other and for all* (1 Thes 5:14–15).

For reflection

• Do you have, or have you had, a close friend to share spiritual experiences with?

• Read and reflect on the book of Sirach, noting the verses about true friendship.

• Name someone, living or dead, famous or not, to whom you would feel drawn for spiritual guidance. Why? (This is a good exercise to do in a small group.)

Chapter Twelve

Fasting

*B*ut when you fast, anoint your head and wash your face, so that you may not appear to be fasting, except to your Father who is hidden.

—Matthew 6:17–18

Passing up food is not the only form of fasting; however, it is one of the basic ways. There is something truly mystical that happens when we allow our bodies to be hungry. When we are satisfied, we usually don't go looking for more. Deep inside each person is a niche that only God can fill. So by allowing ourselves to be empty, we make a place for God to enter in.

While fasting may also be good for the waistline,

the true effect happens in our hearts. *Yet even now, says the LORD,/return to me with your whole heart,/with fasting, and weeping, and mourning;/Rend your hearts, not your garments,/and return to the LORD, your God* (Jl 2:12–13). Rend our hearts. Tear our hearts wide open for the love of God. Fasting facilitates this rending.

George Maloney, author of *A Return to Fasting*, reminds us that in order for fasting to have spiritual effects, it must lead us to an openness to love and serve our neighbors.[27] All spiritual practices should draw us closer to God's love, which will overflow in sharing that love with those around us.

Fasting and abstinence "help us acquire mastery over our instincts and freedom of heart."[28] Of course, we can fast from many things: television, desserts, movies, expensive vacations, gossip, negative thoughts, criticism, nagging. Whenever we make a conscious decision to make room for the LORD, even in a small way, it has big results in our spiritual lives.

"To fast in a personalized, Christian way," Father Maloney reflects, "one needs to consult the Holy Spirit constantly."[29] This advice is helpful because God may not be calling us to fast from all food for a set number of days. Maybe he is calling us to fast from one meal a day for a few days or from snacking between meals. By starting with limited fasting, we can experience success and slowly allow ourselves to be more open to God's prompting.

Think about your own life. Have you ever thought about fasting one day per year for each of your children? Or for your parents? What about a family day of fasting for someone in your parish who is ill or struggling? Brainstorming with your family might start a family tradition with great spiritual power.

The season of Lent is the traditional time for fasting and abstinence. Preparation for Christ's death and resurrection demands some additional sacrifice and further attention to how we stand before the Lord. We can enter that season with joy in knowing that by suffering with Jesus, we are deepening our commitment to unity with God. Remember, that is the goal.

Fasting can also be useful before making decisions, starting a new service project, or going on a retreat. Before sending Barnabas and Saul on to missionary work from Antioch, the community fasted and prayed. *Then, completing their fasting and prayer, they laid hands on them and sent them off* (Acts 13:3).

For reflection

• Discern one area in your life where it might be spiritually useful to fast periodically.

• What roadblocks come up when you try to fast? How do you handle them?

• List some ways society makes it difficult to fast.

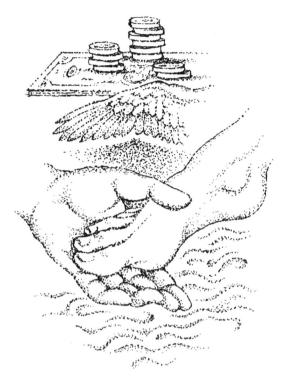

thirteen
fourteen
fifteen

Chapter Thirteen
Stewardship

*E*ach must do as already determined,
without sadness or compulsion, for
God loves a cheerful giver.
                              –2 Corinthians 9:7

To give back to God a portion of what we have received is good spiritual training in trust. *Honor the* LORD *with your wealth,/with first fruits of all your produce;/Then will your barns be filled with grain,/with new wine your vats will overflow* (Prv 3:9–10). We should always strive to keep the importance of material wealth in our lives in perspective and to be unselfish in sharing our wealth with the community and with those in need. Recall the widow who gave the only penny she had (Mk 12:41–44).

We gain valuable insights into our spiritual progress when we can let money come and go, trusting that God will always take care of us. There are many areas in our lives that are more important than money. *No one can serve two masters. He will either hate one and love the other, or be devoted to one and despise the other.* You cannot serve God and mammon (Mt 6:24).

Often the riches we share with others will come back to us in wonderful and surprising ways. For example, a Dominican nun who lives in a monastery of cloistered sisters, was in charge of the kitchen at one point. Since the community had to rely heavily on donations in order to survive, caring individuals and businesses were constantly bringing food to their door. She recalls that as she shared the very best of what came to her door with five or six needy families, the volume and quality of what came from others increased correspondingly. Less is often more.

This concept can also apply to our daily lives. Jesus calls us all to a simple life. Our society does not make it easy. Advertisements are constantly bombarding us with messages that we need more of everything. The implication is that more possessions will make us happy. But the message of God is very different. *Be it little or much, be content with what you have* (Sir 29:23).

It is easier to focus on what is truly important when we realize that God owns everything. We have only been given a temporary loan. God has the rights to it; we have the responsibility for it. In his book *Master Your Money*, Ron Blue recommends that when we are making decisions about spending our money, we should consider each financial decision to be a spiritual decision.[30] *Dispose of your treasure as the Most High commands,/for that will profit you more than the gold* (Sir 29:11).

Many people see no connection between their spiritual lives and their money. Philip Lenihan, founder of Financial Foundations for the Family, reflects that we have a brick wall between our faith and our finances.[31] If our financial lives are not in good working order, we will not be able to advance in our spiritual lives.

We need to spend our money wisely, and not just on tithing and giving to the poor. We need to make every dollar count. Sit down with your family sometime and make a list of things you buy that are not important when viewed through the lens of eternity. How much of it could you do without? *Why spend your money for what is not bread; your wages for what fails to satisfy? Heed me, and you shall eat well, you shall delight in rich fare* (Is 55:2).

Raising our children with the idea that God and people are more important than money is invaluable spiritually. Using our money with an eye to stewardship of the resources God has loaned to us will strengthen our spiritual walk with Jesus.

Tell the rich in the present age not to be proud and not to rely on so uncertain a thing as wealth but rather on God, who richly provides us with all things for our enjoyment. Tell them to do good, to be rich in good works, to be generous, ready to share, thus accumulating as treasure a good foundation for the future, so as to win the life that is true life (1 Tm 6:17–19).

For reflection

• Name one thing that you could do to simplify your life right now.

• What are your fears about tithing or giving? What might have caused those fears?

• Can you recall an experience in which you felt that God blessed you for giving?

Chapter Fourteen

Service

H e said in reply, "You shall love the Lord, your God, with all your heart, with all your being, with all your strength, and with all your mind, and your neighbor as yourself."

—Luke 10:27

Ultimately, our journey inward should bring us to service and social action. A healthy spiritual life will be a balance of inner prayer and outer service. God calls us to love our neighbors by serving them in one way or another.

We may be one to sow the seeds, water the plants, or harvest the crop—each of us has our own niche. *As a body is one though it has many parts, and all the parts of the* body, though many, are one body, so also Christ (1 Cor 12:12). Sometimes responding to God's call to serve can be scary, but St. Paul reassuringly reports that God does not call the qualified, he qualifies the called (2 Cor 3:5-6).

St. Bernard of Clairvaux says that most Christians act as canals for God's love. But what God really needs us to be is reservoirs. So his advice is, "First be filled, and then control the outpouring. The charity that is benign and prudent does not flow outwards until it abounds within."[32]

In other words, we should allow God to fill us completely, and then our service will just be the overflow of God's love within us. And we can't neglect keeping ourselves filled by daily prayer, retreat, Eucharist, and other spiritual practices.

Bob Mumford, in a wonderful book called *Take Another Look at Guidance,* eloquently weaves Scripture into practical guidelines for learning to perceive God's movement and call. He outlines the three harbor lights that help us to know whether God is really asking us to serve in the way we are considering: (1) Is it scriptural? Does it go against biblical principles? Anything that does is not from God. (2) Did a prompting from the Holy Spirit come? Did we have a dream or receive a letter, or did someone ask us to get involved? (3) Have circumstances lined up to confirm the prompting? Waiting is often the hardest part. But rushing to do God's will before the time is right can be devastating.[33]

Look at the story of Moses. He felt God's indignation at how the Israelites were being treated, and he physically lashed out to right some of the wrongs forced on his people. So he heard God's call. But then God whisked him off to the desert to tend sheep for forty years. Moses needed training, molding, and patience. Then God called him back and told him to lead the people out of Egypt. Sometimes we too need that training time before acting on God's will for us.

We can use Mumford's guidelines for discerning where and when God wants us to serve, but we must also focus on serving and loving in our everyday, routine existence. Do we pray for those we live with and work with? Jesus says, *If I, therefore, the master and teacher, have washed your feet, you ought to wash one another's feet* (Jn 13:14).

Are we friendly and open to those God puts in our path—even though we would never choose them for ourselves? In the April 1 reflection of Oswald Chambers' classic *My Utmost for His Highest,* he mused that "God continually introduces us to people in whom we have no interest, and unless we are worshipping God the natural tendency is to be heartless toward them."[34] Chance encounters don't happen. God arranges all our experiences to draw us closer to him, so we can't dismiss even one of those uninteresting people. *Let mutual love continue. Do not neglect hospitality, for through it some have unknowingly entertained angels* (Heb 13:1-2).

Our service must be unselfish. St. Paul reminds us in Galatians 6:3-5: *For if anyone thinks he is something when he is nothing, he is deluding himself.* Although it is a constant challenge in this human condition to think only of God and our neighbor in our ministry, we must continually work at it. The challenge is to allow God to work through us and give him the glory.

So then you are no longer strangers and sojourners, but you are fellow citizens with the holy ones and members of the household of God (Eph 2:19). Literally losing ourselves in the love and service of God will result in union with the living God. And that is the goal.

For reflection

• Where or how is God calling you to serve right now?

• Reflect on one of these scripture passages about service: John 13:1–15, Ephesians 4:1–16, Hebrews 13:1–3, James 2:14–26, 1 Peter 4:7–11.

• What weakness in you or in your life may hold you back from giving yourself into the service of God?

Chapter Fifteen

Listening

I will listen for the word of God;/surely the
Lord will proclaim peace/To his people,
to the faithful,/to those who trust in him.
    —Psalm 85:9

Whatever prayer mode or spiritual practices we
use, listening for God's response to us should be a priority.
Mother Teresa wrote, "I always begin my prayer in silence,
for it is in the silence of the heart that God speaks."[35] Let us
take the time to be still and listen to God. *How precious is
your steadfast love, O God!/All people may take refuge in the
shadow of your wings./They feast on the abundance of your
house;/and you give them drink from the river of your*

delights./For with you is the fountain of life;/in your light we see light (Ps 36:7–10).

Samuel heard the voice of God during the quiet of night: *When Samuel went to sleep in his place, the LORD came and revealed his presence, calling out as before, "Samuel, Samuel!" Samuel answered, "Speak, for your servant is listening"* (1 Sm 3:9–10). Morton Kelsey tells the story of how for many years, he would wake up in the night, unable to get back to sleep. Finally, a psychiatrist friend told him, "Maybe God is trying to get your attention. He did it for Samuel, why not for you?" Although he was skeptical, the next night Morton got out of bed and waited for God to speak to him. And he did. For over thirty years now, God has been speaking to Morton in the middle of the night when all else is silent.[36] God's voice is constantly speaking. Are we listening? Are we tuned in to his frequency?

God may speak to us during the night or through our daily tasks. *For God is the one who, for his good purpose, works in you both to desire and to work. Do everything without grumbling or questioning* (Phil 2:13–14). That means everything—paperwork, housework, commuting. Jesus walks with us and whispers his love to us even in our mundane daily activities. *"Come," my heart says, "seek his face"! Your face, LORD, do I seek* (NRSV, Ps 27:8). God's face is deep in our prayer time, but he stands smiling in the midst of ordinary time as well. Simply recognizing his presence can sanctify every detail of our lives.

If we are lucky, some part of our day or night brings us in contact with a flower, a sunset, springtime blossoms, a gentle rain, warm sunshine, or a starlit sky.

The signature of God is written over all of creation. Let us take the time to soak in the glory of our world. *The clear vault of the sky shines forth like heaven itself, a vision of glory./ The orb of the sun, resplendent at its rising:/what a wonderful work of the Most High!...Behold the rainbow! Then bless its Maker,/for majestic indeed is its splendor;/It spans the heavens with its glory,/this bow bent by the mighty hand of God* (Sir 43:1–2, 11–12).

And finally, let us listen to God's voice in our service to others. *Instruct me, O LORD, in the way of your statues,/that I may exactly observe them. Give me discernment, I that may observe your law,/and keep it with all my heart./Lead me in the path of your commands,/for in it I delight* (Ps 119:33–35). Alone we can do nothing. If we serve always with an ear for the Lord's wisdom and leading, grace will pour forth in power from the depths of the Holy Trinity. *The voice of the LORD is over the waters;/the God of glory thunders,/the LORD, over the mighty waters./The voice of the LORD is powerful;/the voice of the LORD is full of majesty* (NRSV, Ps 29: 3-4).

As mentioned earlier, a healthy spiritual life will be a balance of inner prayer and outward service to our neighbor. It's a glorious path to walk! To drink deeply from the river of prayer, to be anchored in the kingdom of God, to work toward union with the living God—that is the goal. *Happy are those/who do not follow the advice of the wicked/or take the path that sinners tread,/or sit in the seat of scoffers;/ but their delight is in the law of the LORD/and on his law they meditate day and night./They are like trees/planted by streams of water,/which yield their fruit in its season,/and their leaves do not wither. In all that they do, they prosper* (NRSV, Ps 1:1–3).

Brother Lawrence exhorts, "Anyone is capable of a very close and intimate dialogue with the Lord. It is true, some find it easier than others. But remember, the Lord knows that fact too! So begin. Whether you are one who finds this easy or difficult is not important. Begin. He knows which category you are in! It just may be that He is waiting for a resolution on your part to start. So make that resolution. Now!"[37]

May the eyes of [your] hearts be enlightened, that you may know what is the hope that belongs to his call, what are the riches of glory in his inheritance among the holy ones, and what is the surpassing greatness of his power for us who believe (Eph 1:18–19).

Notes

1. *Catechism of the Catholic Church (CCC)*, (English translation), Washington, D.C.: United States Catholic Conference, Inc.—Libreria Editrice Vaticana, 1994, 2697.

2. Brother Lawrence and Frank Laubauch, *Practising His Presence*. (Sargent, GA: Christian Books, 1973), p. 25.

3. CCC, 2725.

4. Susan Muto, *Late Have I Loved Thee: The Recovery of Intimacy*. (New York: Crossroad, 1995), p. 60.

5. Kevin Irwin, *Liturgy, Prayer, and Spirituality*. (Mahwah, NJ: Paulist Press, 1984), p. 298.

6. Fr. Jack Spaulding, *Hope for the Journey*. (Santa Barbara, CA: Queenship Publishing Co., 1995), p. 65.

7. Robert DeGrandis, S.S.J., *Healing Through the Mass*. (Williston Park, NY: Resurrection Press, 1992), pp. 73-74.

8. Scott and Kimberly Hahn, *Rome Sweet Home*. (San Francisco: Ignatius Press, 1993), p. 147.

9. CCC, 1468.

10. Dennis and Matthew Linn, *Healing of Memories: Prayer and Confession Steps to Inner Healing.* (Mahwah, NJ: Paulist Press, 1984), p. 70.

11. Mary Hartman, "The News" (song), 1985.

12. Morton Kelsey, *Companions on the Inner Way: The Art of Spiritual Guidance.* (New York: Crossroad, 1991), p. 129–130.

13. Philip Zaleski, *The Recollected Heart* (San Francisco: HarperSanFrancisco, 1995), p. 11.

14. Ibid., p 12.

15. CCC, 2705, 2708.

16. Morton Kelsey, *The Other Side of Silence: A Guide to Christian Meditation.* (Mahwah, NJ: Paulist Press, 1976), p. 109.

17. Ibid., p. 125.

18. Ibid., p. 179.

19. CCC, 2710.

20. M. Basil Pennington, O.C.S.O., *Centering Prayer: Renewing an Ancient Christian Prayer Form.* (New York: Image Books, 1980).

21. Thomas Merton, *New Seeds of Contemplation.* (New York: New Directions Publishing Corp., 1961), p. 261.

22. John Sanford, *Dreams and Healing.* (Mahwah, NJ: Paulist Press, 1978), p. 11.

23. St. John of the Cross, *Dark Night of the Soul.* (New York: Image Books, 1959), p. 51.

24. Muto, *Late Have I Loved Thee*, p. 20.

25. CCC, 2690.

26. Thomas E. Legere, *Your Spiritual Journey:*

Ancient Truths and Modern Insights. (Liguori, MO: Liguori Publications, 1985), pp. 87–88.

27. George Maloney, *A Return to Fasting.* (Greensboro, NC: Dove Publications, 1974), p. 18.

28. CCC, 2043.

29. Maloney, *A Return to Fasting,* p. 4.

30. Ron Blue, *Master Your Money.* (Nashville, TN: Thomas Nelson Publishers, 1993), p. 21.

31. Phil Lenihan, *Finances for Today's Catholic Family.* (Financial Foundations for the Family, 1996), p. 3.

32. Sermon 18, Bernard of Clairvaux, *Sermons on the Song of Songs.* Trans. by Killian Walsh, Cistercian Fathers Series: No. 4 (Kalamazoo, MI: Cistercian Publications, 1971), 136.

33. Bob Mumford, *Take Another Look at Guidance.* (East Lansing, MI: Life Changers, 1993), p. 87.

34. Oswald Chambers, *My Utmost for His Highest.* (Uhrichsville, OH: Barbour, 1992).

35. Mother Teresa, *A Simple Path.* (New York: Ballantine Books, 1995), p. 7.

36. Kelsey, *The Other Side of Silence,* p. 86.

37. Br. Lawrence and Laubach, p. 76.

ILLUMINATIONBOOKS

Other Books in the Series

Little Pieces of Light...Darkness and Personal Growth
by Joyce Rupp

Lessons from the Monastery That Touch Your Life
by M. Basil Pennington, O.C.S.O.

As You and the Abused Person Journey Together
by Sharon E. Cheston

Spirituality, Stress & You
by Thomas E. Rodgerson

Joy, The Dancing Spirit of Love Surrounding You
by Beverly Elaine Eanes

Every Decision You Make Is a Spiritual One
by Anthony J. De Conciliis with John F. Kinsella

Celebrating the Woman You Are
by S. Suzanne Mayer, I.H.M.

Why Are You Worrying?
by Joseph W. Ciarrocchi

Partners in the Divine Dance of Our Three Person'd God
by Shaun McCarty, S.T.

Love God...Clean House...Help Others
        by *Duane F. Reinert, O.F.M. Cap.*

Along Your Desert Journey
        by *Robert M. Hamma*

Appreciating God's Creation Through Scripture
        by *Alice L. Laffey*

Let Yourself Be Loved
        by *Phillip Bennett*

Facing Discouragement
        by *Kathleen Fischer and Thomas Hart*

Living Simply in an Anxious World
        by *Robert J. Wicks*

A Rainy Afternoon with God
        by *Catherine B. Cawley*

Time, A Collection of Fragile Moments
        by *Joan Monahan*